Juniper Yarnall-Ben

The Capacity of Open Spaces

by

Juniper Yarnall-Benson

For everything cheap incense can't fix

Introduction

By Laurie Parker

When I read the poems in The Capacity of Open Spaces, I felt like I was looking into a kaleidoscope of fractured jewels. Each new poem is a shift in the lens- a whole new dimension revealed. These are well ordered yet explosive pictures, bursts of pain or pleasure. There is also a wandering impulse, a prismatic compass searching for a direction, a young nomad with an old soul trying to find a path through the detritus of the modern world.

Born in November of 2001 Juniper Yarnall-Benson belongs to the first generation coming of age in the third millennium. The poetry collection she's created eighteen years later has a sense of that unusual beginning. So authentic and vulnerable that it feels more like a telepathic communication than a written one.

For an 18-year-old in 2020, all the established roads are in need of maintenance, no clear paths to tread anymore; all formerly 'sure bets' are off. A new migration is underway, a flight from the well-worn past that no longer leads to a predictable future, a tsunami of insurmountable problems carrying everything out to surf. Does this make possible a kind of freedom?

The first line from the first poem in the collection *Slaughterhouse:*

Things happened and I happened with them

The forging of character in the fires of harsh and brutal things resonates throughout this collection.

Life is hard for everyone
Even when everything is okay

There is something essential and immediate reflected in The Capacity of Open Spaces that speaks to the present where digital life is subsuming the material world. Does someone's hands around your neck prove your physical reality? Is a bloody nose evidence of being alive? These poems tell of finding a way with no maps, no guidance, making it all up yourself, a memoir of pain and coming-of-age happening before the reader's eyes.

Slaughterhouse

Things happened and I happened with them
No matter which scenario I play in my head the answer is always the same
"I don't know"
The best I've got right now is doing what I should
Because no matter which song I play in the car, the destination is always the same
Alone, back aching, with a cup of noodles in Fred Meyers
Or trying to sleep on his lap hoping he won't spill that beer
Thinking about how I'm a bad person for letting him kiss me
When really I just regret it because he isn't you
But mostly if we're being honest, I like the way he holds my neck
Like a bird before the slaughterhouse
So I can't run away

Wooden Deck Chairs

Sitting in the same wooden deck chairs I have since childhood
Reading a different book with the same cover
Under the same sun on a different day
Trying to fight off sleep among the seeding kale and peas
In tiny boxes facing my chair
So I can pretend I'm in a vast historical garden
Or maybe back in Costa Rica
Where everything was right but maybe not okay
I drink ginger and turmeric to solve all my problems
And try to stare life straight in the face
Being okay with not knowing what comes next or after that
In the same life on a different day
Someone is mowing and someone else is feeding their cat
"Here kitty kitty, here kitty kitty"
Their voice carries through their small universe to mine
And I recall my last thought as I fell asleep last night
That life is hard for everyone
Even when everything is okay
I patiently await the serious conversation I will have with my mother
In the same tone in a different place
About the future and college and rocket ships
And whether humanity is doomed
Our most bonding moments are always over conflict

In a small restaurant at the wrong time of day
When my mind wanders
To the fact that my legs are now "honey colored" and
I wake up at 8 am
I wonder what it would feel like to be content
While I sit in my overgrown backyard
Dreaming about the same place
On a different day

Coming Home

Home is such a weird concept
A person, a place, a thing,
Completion
There is never completion
Not until death at least
Maybe not even after
How would I know?
Home is peace
Quite
Comfort?
Home is where I hid in the car while strangers talked about my house like it was theirs
When I was just six years old
Home is where I know every rock and tree and brick and stream
Until they all moved on without me
Home is where I sat on the roof in the rain
Lost without the ocean and the silence
That had been my world growing up
Home was a bedroom for a while
Hands, a neck, the smell of laundry detergent
Home was a basement
Five people not really watching the TV
A park bench at night
When it was just a little bit too cold to be summer anymore
Then home slowly walked away from me and I watched them go
And felt him feel nothing when he held me

While I cried in the woods by the river
Pleading for them to come back
Home became a goal
A someday, a maybe.
A light at the end of the tunnel
While I sprinted at top speed
Leaving everything else behind
Home was a piece of paper
White and blank
And a pen in my hand
Home was a town on the coast far far away
With a name that didn't belong to me
In a house that wasn't mine
In a different ocean than the one I knew as a child
And yet feeling right at home
Home was not the house with the purple trim, and two dogs, and a bed in the basement
Home was not the mitch-matched pillows
Or the hops in the yard
Or even my sisters' arms
Because the dogs don't sleep with me anymore
And I wake up to an empty house
Or sit on the skate ramp for hours without moving
Thinking about going home
Home is not this house at the end of a long dirt driveway
On an island in the cold green sea
Home is not these roads and these trees
Because they grew and so did I
But I wasn't here to see it
And even the rocks have moved on without me

Covered in moss and hidden by blackberries
That other little kids pick with their mothers
While I sit on the couch of someone else's living room
Wondering where if anywhere
There is room for me to live

Lifting Weights

There's this weight that I've been carrying
The same one that made him comment on the muscles in my back
During a cold shower in a thunderstorm
In the apartment at the end of the road
"I work out" I said
I lift weights everyday
I don't remember life without them
Although I guess there must have been a few years before the accident
If that really is what caused this

I carried this weight as I watched my brother
Intent and protective
Always worried he'd get lost in the crowd
Grabbing his arm or shoulder
Trying to steer him away
Even then it annoyed him
Not that it ever did us any good

I carried this weight
Right there between my shoulder blades
Like the yolk of an oxen
Or Atlas carrying the world
In the over packed car that my family drove
Down from my quiet world into this loud one
Where everything I did was wrong
From what I wore to how I talked
And even the things I loved

I carried this weight as I carried my little sister
She was a big baby
Through the rooms of my first house in the city
It's crazy to think she hasn't always been here in person
Because I know she's always been in my life

Sometimes I could sit down for a while
Set the weight on one side of the couch
A body on the other
But sometimes the bodies just added to the weight
And I needed to be alone

I never thought about it being there
Just how those who grew up with faith learn not to question it
Or how an addict reaches for a hit without even realizing
Muscle memory
Tight across my back

But the thing about weight is it holds you down
Keeps you grounded
So when someone took the weight away
I was the one who was lost
My singular constant no longer existing
I could be swept away by anything
Lost in the crowd

Costa Rica

My lips feel dry at the sides from the salt
And my hair hangs in almost unrecognizable strands
in my face
While my body sways back and forth from the after
taste of the ocean
The club is empty at noon in the pouring rain
So we have the small outdoor deck to ourselves
While he points out famous surf breaks
And tells me to put the rolling paper under my shirt
to keep it dry

Confessional

A bag of spicy peanuts and a beer
Has heard more stories than the confessional
While acquaintances break bread over sports talk
Sitting in camping chairs on the beach
And commenting on the antics of four boys in a canoe
Or shaky hands, wrinkled from the ocean
Desperately grip the edge of a table
While we order three beers and a coffee
At 11 am

Heist movies

When the value of art
Is no longer measured in beauty
But in money
It stops being art
And becomes a heist movie

Success

Am I successful now
That my mouth tastes like cigarettes at 3am?
Because I can almost kickflip
And my pop shove it is pretty good
Am I successful now that I don't get paralyzed over the bathroom sink
Whenever something doesn't go just right
Or am I successful now
Because I'm miles away
From every fault and fuck up I could think of
Stuffed in my closet in cardboard boxes
And left alone
Am I successful in my disappearing act
A charity benefit, all prepaid?
Did I really leave it all behind
Am successful in the numbers
Little paper bound journals recording every detail
Like the lyrics to a Cigarettes After Sex song
With a few less drugs and a few more words
And no bow before I leave the stage
I've always strived for the top percent
Sometimes with the intent of killing myself through my work
Like every good artist or cult leader
With the worst stomach pains in history
And a bloody lip from CPR
Did I do it right? Did I win?
There's something cathartic about a constant lack of sleep

And fingertips burnt to hell
Limping down Hawthorne at midday
Am I successful now?
Graduated with honors
From a class that doesn't know my name
Just to sleep in a hammock on the beach
Like a vintage airport poster
Selling the un-American dream
Am I successful in my romanticizing of self-destruction?
In my purposeful search for mediocracy?
Did I push everyone away?
My list of day to day activities is longer than my list of friends
And let's not start with the timers and alarms I've set
Everything from 'take rice off stove'
To 'bang head against wall'
At home if my legs aren't burning
I don't deserve to breathe
While I claim that salt water is my only real goal in life
And shove matras down my throat
Stolen from various autobiographies of fucked up individuals
I so desperately strive to be
I danced with a man who worked as a mermaid
And if that doesn't describe my life
I'm not sure what does
Except maybe that one bike ride home in the rain
My red and white shirt ripping
And my keys about to be lost

Am I successful now?
While I eat at Denny's at 1am
Ordering in broken Spanish
And shove my skateboard into the overhead compartment of every plane
I guess it's time to sleep it off in the airport again
And wish I wrote novels like the men in sweaters do
Probably on their way home to Hollywood
To catch their next big break
Or maybe their next ex wife
Am I successful now that I make it home every night?
Because I get enough sleep?
I'm still unhappy
The puritan way
Sounds poetic, doesn't it?

Artists

What's the worst part of being an artist?
Hating everything you create
But needing, on a deep spiritual level
To create it anyways
Comprising between your idea
And what's commonly acceptable
While dreading each and every still life you make
Or maybe it's the desire for *more*
That sits in you constantly
Even in the bath at 10pm
With a bottle in one hand and a book in the other
It might be the self-destructive nature
Of pulling something straight from your heart
And messily smearing it on a page
Or it could be the painful existence
When one is forced to absolutely always tell the truth
Sometimes the worst part of being an artist
Is that something important and beautiful
Is happening all the time
So it's absolutely necessary you go out and find it
Rather than sitting at your desk making art

Phone Tag or 'Porn'

Sometimes it's just easier to give them your number
Than to think of something nice to say
Sometimes the guy who asks you for directions is in his 30s
But he just moved to Portland and is looking for friends!
Sometimes it's my fault for acting like that
For doing what I did
I'm not even going to pretend to make excuses
But that doesn't mean he had to call me nine times
At 8am
Sometimes you strike a casual conversation in person
But somewhere deep down you know
And it ends with a simple invitation to
"Call me if you need anything"
Followed by a text about an hour later
Which leads to questionable things in your search history
And sexting with the translate app
Sometimes it's someone you used to know
Two contacts with the same singular first name
"what's up"
"how're you"
Ok
Please leave me alone
Sometimes it's the camera guy who asked for a photo
With the hula hoop around your waist

Who must have been at least 6'3 and sported a ponytail
Honestly deserving of his own poem
'Porn' I would call it
And it would discuss the hypocritical nature
Of pony tailed men
Who all carry cameras and think what they've got is special
And to whom Portland is the new Hollywood dream

A mango

Cut up and wrapped in an extra plastic bag
A bottle of wine I have yet to open
And a curry like mixture I cooked
And have yet to eat
A singular onion
Red I think
And a pepper shoved in the back
Along with a chocolate wrapper containing one bite sized piece
That I've been saving for
Just the right night

Underwear or an American tourist in Greece

Today I did laundry for the first time
And I can accurately say that nothing else has
solidified so much
The fact that I'm free
There's nothing like the smell of someone else's
laundry detergent
Or sitting on a small plastic chair surrounded by
sheets
While reading a paperback and glancing at the clock
To remind you you're living on your own time
There's nothing like seeing 11 pairs of underwear
Laid out across the backs of chairs in the sun
Each belonging to their own fantasy
Or memory if you're lucky
To make you take a step back and see yourself
From a distance
The nylon ones dry the fastest
And thus are best for travel when you're doing
laundry in a sink
But you've also got two pairs of green
And a fire engine red with only a small rip
Then there's the ones with just a hint of lace
For days when you're feeling flirty
All laid out in stark honest contrast
To the all-white laundry of the woman next door
Whose underwear must cover her waist
Just two pairs, both white
Next to some towels on a clothesline
You saw her earlier

While out doing yoga on your balcony
At none other than 7am
She had a broom and a simple expression
As she opened her window to let in the sun

Paros

It's 4pm and they're already dancing
Stomping and spinning like we did last night
In our all black clothes and foggy minds
To wake up and see stars out of the corner of my eye
Thinking
"What a beautiful way to start the morning"
Their music can be heard all the way across the beach
While plastic bottles of water threaten to blow in the wind
And another couple
Tourists you can tell
Make out in the waist deep water
In the same paradise as the three fishermen
Obviously proud of their small crowd of onlookers
Who wrapped a swordfish in plastic
On my way to the store
And the kid in a red shirt
Paces up and down the beach
Like he has everyday
Accompanied by a vacantly troubled expression
And not wearing shoes

Aesthetics

And then there's the question of aesthetics
Which we discuss heavily at midnight on the wicker chairs outside his house
Me eating a lime popsicle
And him playing Peach Pit on the speakers of his phone
Is a cigarette in the rain
A matter of pleasure or self-destruction?
While one contemplates the sadness of life
Brought on by a break up
We all knew was coming
If that's the truth than we really can't judge him
For the time he took acid and explained the universe in the carpet
While staring at the naked floor
Or the time I showed up at his house
With an ice pack on my neck
That I stole from a Chinese restaurant in the mall
And we talked for two hours with the television on
While our siblings tried to kill themselves upstairs

Off Season

That September
I wore a wool sweater that made my arms itch
On the bus in the rain
And he wore a windbreaker
A grey one like he always did
We all needed haircuts
And to not talk so loud
But it was hard to stay silent while intoxicated
By the welcome pressure of each other's presence
And the windows covered in steam
Bright red for the stop lights at rush hour
As I brushed garlic from my pant legs
And played STFKR over the loudspeakers at work

Last September
I cradled bruised knuckles
While he put out his cigarette on the side of a
Mexican food truck
And I shifted from foot to foot
Living off my thermos of black coffee
In a sweatshirt way past the time it was warm enough
With high socks to cover my ankles
Because I didn't want to draw attention
And I needed to hide the scars

Fuck Buddies

Face down in his sheets
Next to her in bed
He used to tell me he couldn't sleep alone
Sometimes I wondered if that's why he made it quick
She chewed mint gum while I kissed her
And made empty promises
So we could both pretend what he did was okay
And now I think I appreciate that book so much
Because I know the pressure of weight
And the pain of lightness
Or rather lightheadedness
That I found through each cigarette
So I didn't need to remember him
Force feeding me butter on the basement floor

Housewife Fantasy

My dad's best friend told him
That the greatest way his children could rebel
Was by getting a degree and buying a suit
So maybe it was subconsciously
That I submitted myself to you
Because surrendering my independence for your enjoyment
Was the kinkiest thing I knew how to do

Intimate Moments

The end of a paperback novel
My fingertips dry and covered in salt
The smell of coconut oil coming from every corner
And my feet hurt from walking so far
I wonder what my grandma sees when she looks in the mirror like I do
There's something in my bloodline that says
"Keep walking"
And we all walk too fast for our own good
When my sister was younger we would take her in the stroller
And I would run every other step to keep up
Sometimes she would kick off her shoes to stop us
Even then reminding me to take it easy
Slow it down
I wonder how Atlas feels when he looks in the mirror
Does he cringe at the way his muscled arms look
In comparison to his arched and aching back?
Does he lay flat in his white bedroom
Contemplating the investment of a bottle of gin
To fulfill the fantasy
Of loving alone?
A scribbled note in the corner of a novel
"The prophet was never happy"
And each morning I feel more and more like my mother
And hate it less and less
Much to the distain of 14-year-old me

Who still lives in the train yard with a bag of cookies and red hair
I swing back and forth from guilt to gratitude
Like any soldier with bloody hands
Who by some dumb luck is still alive
"Maybe you can live like that for a while but it can't last forever"
My aching feet say forever is a bad word
So I choose tape over glue
And never look back
This is my dry lipped rambling
From the intimate moments
Conceived of black nail polish and the knowledge that someday
I'll receive her encouraging words
But until then I have my half hour naps
In which I never close my eyes part II
And write in mores code just to please myself
Because I'm mysterious
Badass and lonely
And definitely not see through

Conditions

And once again
Like all those before me
The decisions that make me happy
Separate me from everyone else
So I can follow in those footsteps
Of the artists living for substance
And the journalists whose story trumps their lives
And join my family in their ornate gold towers
Barefoot and lonely
To the scent of imported incense
And expensive habits
The product of back breaking labor
Leaving us empty
The palace of our lives.

Grieving

I miss her
I miss her loud voice and short shorts
I miss her obsession with pineapple sour patch kids
And the night she hula hooped on the table to please the crowd
I miss the way she always ran, never walking
And the way she would cry while she argued
Because everything mattered so much
I miss her schizophrenic playlists
How hard she would slap him
And the long walks home in the rain
I miss the nights she spent on the phone
Finding every argument to make him stay
I miss the day she washed her shirt in his bathroom sink
And the way she wrapped her fist around the knife
I miss her bruised legs and the way she paid with quarters
And always left the movie playing
I miss the green sheets
And the way her sweater smelled
I miss when she came home covered in mud
And spent the rest of the day playing solitaire
And crying because she knew it could never last

Sapling

I refused to get off the trampoline
And come inside
"God damn you're stubborn"
He told me and I was furious
Because I might not know the definition of the world but
I am not!
"Being stubborn is a good thing. It's like being a tree"
But I was beyond consoling
And fumed about it all day

Guilty Pleasure meet Self Control

I'm trying to be as empty as I feel
Shouldn't I be full?
Everyone has to have a breaking point
I taste blood and it's a familiar feeling
But familiar doesn't always mean comfortable
A perfect machine
Without a brain
Or was it a heart?
I don't remember
Why *did* the Tin Man have a brain?
It's the human condition
Feed the brain! Feed it!
Have I lost touch with reality or just myself?
Never mind
I am reality
"Good morning! Welcome home!"
I think I might be in hibernation
Hibernation?
No. Chrysalis
Are you exhausted from mental exercise?
I think I might have pulled a muscle
Am I growing or shrinking?
The very hungry caterpillar
Who grew up and starved itself
For enlightenment
And The Greater Good
So why is no one answering?
"You lead an awfully mental life"
I don't want to sleep anymore

But I don't want to sleep with just anyone
Of course I miss him
You can't play tricks on me!
Familiar doesn't always mean comfortable
And maybe It's just because I love mourning
Mornings
Spontaneous insanity
As pen meets ripped page
As tongue meets teeth
As heart meets brain
Perpetual indulgence
What would she say if she saw me now?
"Wow you're so tan"
Probably

She

The first time I fell in love
She was a girl
And neither of us knew what it meant
The night she asked me to sleep on the couch with her
Rather than get out the guest bed
And we lay side by side, or bodies fitting perfectly
Trying not to fall off
Just a sleepover, just friends
Neither of us knew what it meant
The night I had a concussion
And I kissed her shoulder while she slept
She squeezed my hand and I pretend she was still asleep
So neither of us needed to know what it meant
Neither of us knew what it meant when I mouthed the words "I love you"
Just to see how it sounded
How it felt
My lips against her skin
Neither of us knew what it meant
So we both left bruises
From various abusive games
And the longer we loved the darker they got
Saying "This is mine"
She was mine
As over takeout pizza and bagels after sleepless nights
I put my head on her shoulder in the car

And we sat closer and closer on the basement floor
Definitely watching Dirty Dancing
And not each other from the corners of our eyes
Neither of us knew what it meant
When she tackled me during our most heated argument
And held me and didn't let go
With her chin on my head and her arms around my chest
And I let her
And we lay like that all night
Neither of us knew what it meant
The day she took me to her country club
Where all you had to do was give your last name
And white shirted officials showed up with scented soap and ice cream bars
I put my arms around her in the pool
Her skin cool and wet and smelling of chlorine
In front of everyone
Thinking over and over
"We're just friends"
When she got in a fight on the soccer field
I took the punches like always
But afterwards they told me
"Go get your girlfriend"
And she stared me straight in the eyes
But I looked away
And we both knew what it meant

Paris

The same bakery with the same faded ceiling
The same chicken sandwich with just the right amount of mayo
Wrapped in the same wrinkled paper
The cooler whirs on and the clicks off again
And the angry looking woman behind the counter
Flips the electrical switch with tongs
And I think
I will probably always be alone
But I don't mind
I think maybe I enjoy solitude more
When surrounded by voices that don't know me
In tongues I can't understand
Having conversations I can only imagine
So instead I'm an outsider
An onlooker, an alien
Exotic
In my leather jacket
But only poetically so
On a pilgrimage to save the world
By running and hiding behind little black books
Bound in Chinese factories
And forgotten on deli floors

A Crash Course on Everything

Red hot desire
On the back burner of my eyes
They say everything looks uglier up close
But in the small round mirror I look severe
And it's hard to hate something so intimately
When hate can so often be love
I take dietary advice from Ernest Hemingway
And his movable feast
While feasting my eyes on hunger and starvation
And the severity of skin and bone
I smell like honey to save the bees
Barefoot on the tile floor
And want so badly to be honest
But the pathological liar in me stays awake
And all I can do is shake my head
I am the walls I build no matter how beautiful
Their purpose is still
To keep you away

Teargas

Baggy sweaters baggy eyes
I am coming home late
Alone
We never kiss goodbye
We're all in love
White underwear
Arms wide
Fingertips inches from a glass
The contentment of a headache
And a breath of fresh air
I am strong, I am wrapped in layers of cotton
I am eating burnt toast and drinking from the coffee pot
I cover my aching body in a jacket and in bitterness
You are crying

A Miracle

Someone once asked me
Drunk, on a balcony in Greece
"Have you ever seen a miracle?"
He said it like it was urgent
And I think he repeated it twice
As to be heard over the general rowdiness of the conversation
Or lack thereof that filled the room
I didn't need to answer because no one cared
And someone else yelled from the room above
But in the small basement of a hotel in Paris
It ate at me
And I remembered

A yellow shirt in the rain
A green picnic table
We made awkward eye contact over a cheekbone
That made you smile lip to lip
And finally there was someone
Who looked me in the eye
Out in the open
Like art on a wall
Saying look
This is something worth seeing
No matter how up close
And dirty
You get

Redeye

Even here in this city so full of life
Like a living breathing body
Of warped roads and sweet-smelling chestnuts
Where people in winter jackets of all colors
Hurry back and forth between cigarettes
Walking their small dogs and fervent lovers
I find myself receding
While desperately holding eye contact
With my own reflection in the cheese shop window
While we wait to cross the street
I find any excuse to get away
A moment in the tiny elevator
The back of my neck tingling
Eyes wandering to the other side of the park
The only real way to see things
Through my eyes alone
My brain spilling narrative after narrative
Sitting dead eyed in a cafe
Staring off into the distant street
Thinking please
Just shut up

Push Ups

On a park bench in the wind
Brown leaves noisily
Making their way across the street
The coffee is warm in the pit of my stomach
And the wind is cold on my face
Spring is the time for birth
Because fall is for lovers
And popcorn and nuts and the bitter aftertaste
A prophet sits on a bench
And sings broken verses of reggae songs
While I realize love is not bruised knees
And I don't want it anymore
The hotter the showers I take and the softer the beds I sleep in
The more and more my feet hurt
Just how the more
He looked at me lovingly
The less I could meet his eyes
So I turned my head away
And leaned into him as I would a wall
Now I do push-ups on the hotel room floor
With the windows open and the winter air blowing in
Because Paris is for lovers
And I do not belong here

Spineless Desire

I am a stomach ache
And I don't want to be in love
Kick me please
I am your stray
Limping wet through the backstreets of your life
I will make my bed and lay in it too
And bare my teeth to show my love
But I am not smiling

1pm Watchdog

My favorite feeling was afterwards
When you would fall back asleep
And I would pretend I was too
But in reality I was listening to your breathing
Your dog
In more ways than one
I lay at the foot of your bed
And watched you

Contentment!

Paying with a 50 for a drink on the beach
Bleached hair fading under the sun
A leather jacket over small shoulders
And a weary smile into the distance
The kind you might give to an old acquaintance
You pass on the street
But don't know well enough to say
"Hello"

A plane ticket printed on already used paper
A half-naked bed, and a dish full of ash on the floor
Leaning out of the window in a hotel room to smell the sunset
Or rain and fryer oil
Cracked teeth and bloody socks
From walking and walking and walking
Missing a flight to write poems on an airport carpet
Welcoming warmth of black coffee and dry toast
And a not so cautious descent
Into the unknown

Airplane Food

A watered-down hot chocolate
Eyelids made of lead
I threaten to enjoy myself
As she grabs my arm when the gun goes off
I limp in and out of the bakery
Cross eyes with stale gum
Hardtack and hard candy
And a scalpel on my chest
I set my cracked and broken phone case
On the tile table
And order bo bun and an extra pair of chopsticks
My ankle screams in protest
So I leave my socks on in the shower

Contradictions

I want
A dual life
The intellectual intercourse
Of following you through the museum in the rain
Watching the muscles in your neck through the glass case of the Egyptian exhibit
While making off handed comments
About the philosophical conversation we were having a moment ago
I am stalking my prey
Through dark hallways
Each step soft and deliberate
To keep the exact right distance between us
Without being to close

And the physical pleasure
Of standing on the beach before a storm
Watching the grey waves and white water
Mind racing and heart slow
Pumping blood through veins open from the forest floor
Going at it like animals
Without an ounce of love

Neon Poetry

I want to sleep in this hotel bed
Forever
And cultivate various personalities
With my eyes closed
What is satisfaction? Wine drunk is just a headache
Life will always be hard
And someday my hands will shake like my mom's do
But I can't tell if it's sad
Or beautiful
That she picks up more men than me
Mother daughter bonding
I need something to bite down on
A horse at a bit
Growing up just means learning what you enjoy is unacceptable
Unsustainable
And that self-destruction
Has always been self-love

Polyamory

I have always wanted a simple life that I have never been cut out for
What kind of problem is that
Being in love with too many places?
That was always his problem, not mine
Little did I know
That seeing that ring on his finger
Around her hand
Or his hands, lifting the bong to her dainty lips
And her teeth marks
On his neck
Were signs we were meant for each other
Constantly looking for the next best place
The dip in my collar bone
The cigarette burn halfway up his wrist
A rainy street behind a church
A coast before a storm
The smell of dirt or salt or rotting fruit
Countless hotel rooms
Countless mouths
Always searching for the perishable
I wonder where he is now
I am in the constant state of discontentment
Full but ravenous
A black hole with so much to give

Things that I consume:

Oxygen
Information
My body
Other people's bodies
Coffee
Alcohol
Vices

Things that consume me:

Time
Desire
The constant fear of inadequacy

Comedy

I am the stand-up comedy of the world
As the blind lead the blind and I learn to drink from alcoholics
I am no longer a Doberman
Or a race horse
I am a canvas bag of laundry
Being dragged through the street
Only half full
But unable to carry more
I think the world is getting bigger
But I am shrinking

Genocide

Dispelled form my body
A sense of purging
The lining of my stomach
The bad thoughts
Genocide
It's something we don't talk about
The people that we kill
The girl in the hammock
Her black hair stringy and wet
Her hands around a cup of tea
My sense of comfort
In a world of chaos
Remember how I said I hated it?
"The chaos or the comfort?"
You would ask me
And I would say
I don't know
I run from the chaos
But the comfort has more violence
In hands I cannot bear to hold

A dog barking in a silent country

Intimate views of faraway people
I thought I would end up somewhere
But I am just walking
Empty
Feeling empty
Full
Full of life
Full of experience
A glass full of water
Wine
Two empty glasses of whisky
For the American ladies at the bar
Simplicity of rolling hills
The goats don't scream shut up
And milk flows easily
When emotional satisfaction leads to the physical
Without needing to rely on desire
Open spaces
A warm heart
An open heart, an open door
Open heart surgery
A car above a chasm
And a girl who wishes they will crash
Screaming turkeys
Drunken giggles
I am too sober for life
Always too sober I have no moral obligation
To happiness
Or drowning in this lake

I can be without trauma and not be judged for it
The dissipation of living
Free of the shackles of love I can happily disappear
Into these open spaces

A closed box in an open space
What does it mean?
An overbearing sense of privacy?
An overbearing mother?
The sweet stink of mud
I have morals but no boundaries
It's not mud
It's goats
Who never tell me to shut up because they aren't listening
My perfect audience
Who has no clue I'm on the stage
Stage fright
Open spaces
I could swim forever

I can speak but refuse to entertain
Where am I going?
Open spaces choking on feathers
Plucked from the turkeys
Plucked from the laughter
Shoved down my throat
I have no fear of being insatiable
But I loathe desire
Want me without wanting me
Conundrum

Catastrophe
The capacity
Of open spaces

Symphony

And I love the way you echo
In faint rap music
And the lack of noise
But the groaning of the couch
And our bodies.
It was the most beautiful symphony you ever wrote
The cacophony is catching
Let this silence be our song

Still

Losing myself
Moving myself
Tectonic plates in motion

Castaway

Today I am preparing for a long hard life
Over a bowl of granola and a paperback book
As I take the weight from my shoulders
And the crown from my head
Shoving them deep in my carry-on bag
Set on now
Carrying only a knife
And revering the scars
Why choose bare feet?
Over the comforts of hotel slippers?
Because I crave the blunt force trauma
Of honesty
And cast away
The ten-hour time difference
Of love

Is happiness a full stomach?

Stories of consumption and starvation
That's all we really are
Grown up
Filled up
Allowed to be full
I'm learning to love what I'm consuming
The jury is still out on morality
But my tongue has learned to enjoy the pallet
And I just want to say something other than, "I miss you"
But I have always been in love with nihilists
I am a black hole I am but not dizzy
And I crave the silence found in an abundance of noise
Obsession is a straight line
The kind you learn about in geometry
With a million points but no beginning or end
And I have never been able to breathe
Always trying to catch up with myself
A love affair with emptiness
I will never reach its end or it's beginning
And I just want to be
Like a statue
As she said, I feel myself turning to stone
And have never been more reliable
With my name carved in the pedestal
I become a constant
I have lived a million lives
Let me soak into you

To dissipate myself
In my constant search to find violence
In even the softest things
The rams fleece may have been golden
But all bones bleach the same

Intimacy without Honesty

A married couple
Moved into an old folks' home
And she told him
"Just like everyone else
you become sick of my monotony
And ask for the insides
The blood and the guts"
"But please" he said
"Make it beautiful."

A bucket full of bones

They fake orgasms on the porch
While I drink orange juice from the carton
And draw circles with my teeth
Collective insufficiency
I stand barefoot on broken glass
This is holy ground
But no matter how many times I scream
Into this pastel blue towel
No one is listening
So I'm left to my own devices
And my bucket full of bones

Monday Night Drinking Games

You can probably hear them laughing
All the way down the street
And here I am
Freezing
Her voice sounds shrill after a few drinks
And what good would sleep do
Against this kind of exhaustion?
I need spiritual remedies or maybe a few bruises
So the letters stop moving and the numbers stand still
Have you had your fun with my honesty?
Like a cat and a dead mouse
Batting from eye to eye
How do you make language sound disgusting?
I want to display to you your ignorance
But my future calls in a pair of sandals I left on the beach
Where entirely alone I felt less lonely
Than legs up over that white chair
And my head always down
My voice has never been the quietest in the room
But I have no desire to shout
And I'm sick of my materialistic nature
But cannot share what I do not own
With both eyes closed I pray over a cup of American coffee
And learn to bite my tongue
While denying myself satisfaction
Of the pain

Fictionalized

Kitten season, cancer patient
My life has become more and more fictionalized
I wrote in the corner of a notebook
The formula for any good story
But I am none of those things
I am just a girl on the beach
Who longs to be all three
I have always meant to write
About general unrest in the world
And tried to make myself a character
A protagonist
A narrator
A heroine you could say
Whose life unfolds like carefully constructed origami
Against the cement backdrop of life
I meant to be the voice of reason
Preaching my philosophy between the cracks
Picking apart the details of my sexual and personal exploits
Across the map that is my overly abundant life
But every time I sit down to write about unrest and anarchy
I turn the page to a loaf of bread
And the fact that he set a salt shaker
Full of cinnamon
On the table
I keep meaning to write about cultures and violence
But from my pen comes the incoherent ramblings
Of someone too busy reading to write

Of a tongue too busy tasting to eat
And a bed too hard to sleep on

Madonna and Child

I walked into that church with a bottle of bleach
And thought of the women
I have been afraid of my whole life
On a beach in my hometown
I drew a card from a pile and jokingly asked
How to balance my life
And not be afraid of femininity
Now I stand on a beach
Flies biting at my ankles
And hear the words I've been too afraid to say
I lay warm stones on her back
And shivered
And tore mango from the skin with my teeth
Swatting at yellow jackets
Now swatting at flies
I stand in the church and beg
Afraid of forgiveness
And unwilling to be free
There's an orange tree outside
And the faces of various saints glance at me in agony
Saying
"Let yourself go"
But I'm not one of you and I enjoy my martyrdom
With my bucket of bleach to wash myself clean
She is not everything but she might be something
A glimpse in the ornate mirror that hangs on the wall
We walked for hours with the historic city as our backdrop

And in a tiny cafe
British themed
I ate from your salad and you
Watched the nuns across the street
Who posed for the camera
Like the pictures on these walls
Crying
I have never seen you like that
"Impassible"
I think
As my feet clad in skate shoes march to the beat of a drum
That I've always been playing
When stripped of the metaphors I define myself by
I remember the garage door opening and you crying and I
Feeling nothing
I did not come here to confess my sins
I watch small schools of fish breach the surface
And wonder if they are the fingertips of the woman
With kelp for hair
Yet another martyr for whom I've felt disdain
And yet another woman who I've turned my back on
Sleeping with her in the attic
We laughed and closed the curtains and pretended not to hear
The voices that are all too loud now
Echoing through this chapel
The hum of a finger
Methodically moving around a bottle of beer
The awkward clatter of an old pickup truck

And a sleeping bag in the back of a U-Haul
Floors made of bamboo
That were warm under my small feet
And a bed on the floor
Covered in purple sheets and the smell of lavender
I down coffee after coffee and toss the paper cups away
Thinking nothing of how my hands shake
Tomorrow I will go back there
Leave a coin in the slot and light a candle
That I have not stolen
As the morality of evolution hangs heavy over my head
I don't know why I don't believe in anything

October 31st

It's a universal truth that bags under the eyes are strangely sexy
Or at least that's what I tell myself
While cooking beans and singing along to the Front Bottoms
In a French sweater
The most ecstatic I've been
Was after finding that diner coffee
Watered down and burnt to shit
In too large a paper cup
The kind I can really get my hands around

Now I sip it greedily
And run barefoot at the speed of sound
I've had on my list since we first got here
"Stay awake all night just to see what happens"
I think I imagined myself alone in my room
With the balcony doors open
Sitting cross legged on the floor
Writing furious poetry and drinking iced tea
But just yesterday I came to the conclusion
That if I was going to write anymore
I would need to live a little
So I skipped out
For the second time in my life
And spent half an hour swimming in the sea
At the end of October

With a 9-euro bottle of wine
That made me feel expensive
And cold feet
We didn't mean to stay awake
But sometimes conversation carries you
And one thing after another lead
To the only constellation I know by sight
Making its way from his right shoulder to his left
As stars fell from the sky
Or maybe I imagined all but one of them
But it didn't matter because the sun came up eventually
And for some reason all I could think about
Was the box of Halloween colored junior mints
I had in my fridge

The one night of the year
Spider bites on my feet are festive
While I tip the bed frame onto its side
Suddenly weightless without its mattress
Just like I am suddenly weightless without sleep
The new found floor space
Is just what I need to practice my skate tricks
And the sly smile I'll give when you ask me
"What was all that banging?"
And I'll just answer
"I had a fun night."

Intensity

I do not like using the word
Panties
And I don't know how better to describe myself
Than that

TV Girl Days

Fuck
Both shoes untied
Still untied
And a coffee in each hand
Well
I said I missed her
And here she is bruises all up her neck
Staring at the sun and willing it to rise
Reminding herself Milan Kundera says
Never let them spend the night
Things I've learned part three
I prefer to sleep alone

Mosh Pit

The violence of the sensual touch
Of strangers

Body Count

I stand on the roof of the monastery
In a pair of black boots as a fever comes on
And with cracked lips remember a cardboard box
Full of bodies
And the smell that can only be described as death
My chapel is much smaller
With no pink flowers outside and no sweet incense burning
No cardboard box or garbage bag
Only a laundry basket
Propped up against the wall
The smell here is not of death or incense
But of laundry detergent
And is just as eerie
When the door closes
And leaves you alone

I used to think I was an artist

Self-discipline or self-harm?
This is why we deny pleasure
Because I used to think cinnamon was sweet
And sex has broken more earrings than hearts
Yes I smiled and yes I was happy
Braiding his hair in the house of mirrors
But what's important was how good it felt to close the door
And how I can hear them singing
From my sarcophagus
I'm falling asleep as we speak
But for once it doesn't feel like falling
Habitual love
How do you break habits?
Distraction
Repetition
Association
There are still flavors that I can't taste
I was born
In that crowded van and surreal landscape
On the surface of the sun
I buy an espresso for the headache
My pilgrimage is accompanied by the smell of cigarettes and figs
As infant hands covered in rings
Cut their knuckles on stone
And feel nostalgia
For something they can't explain

Breakfast

I feel top heavy
Like my brain defines my body
And leaves my heart behind
I stand in plastic gloves
With a black bandana covering my face
Breathing in death and cleanliness
The antithesis of life
Sometimes I walk without walking
And my hands are defined by the shapes they hold
The Lopez line
The form of bones
Decomposition is the beginning of life

Gin and Juniper

When I was younger my dad would remind me
On days when I didn't know why I was sad
To remember the flavor of brown sugar
Melting on my tongue
And that's the way I felt
As I walked down the dusty road
Past overflowing garbage bins and stray cats
Carrying a bouquet of flowers
Through the land of thirst

Among the bleached bones
We toasted plastic cups
And welcomed the refreshment
Of limes and gin and dates
Because art has always meant excellence
And has always cheated death

I don't think I understood the word
Fulfillment
Until I tasted the freedom of my 6:30 alarm
And waves lapping on the beach
Words from my mother remind me
That I will always be an artist
So I raise my head and my glass
And keeping walking

No one can change the fact
That I was born in the fertile crescent
The Willamette Valley

Where we carve our bodies from the trees
And what better way to realize your potential
Than by becoming an oasis
But it's a lonely job cutting olive branches
To keep doves fed
So I will pluck the feathers
Without asking what you love
Fear me
Or drink alone

Licking sickly sweet candy from my fingers
As the sun goes down
I desire to be draped in jewelry
With chains around my feet
Branded like the skin of horses
And the slaves that lifted these monuments
How many of the world's wonders are burial chambers?
Maybe here
I don't want to be free

Today I eat cake for breakfast
Because the Greeks may not have drunk blood and chocolate
But wine is just as dark
And full is the beginning of fulfillment
Because warm cheeks and cold showers
Are no worse than bruised knees

Sunset

I said earlier today
I liked the word reflective
Because the mirror showed me what I wanted to see
But the real word I think
Is decadence
Because rough sheets can feel like silk
While I eat fruit in bed
Like Cleopatra with the TV on
I share this landscape
With two mothers and two beers
And two young boys with neon shovels
I try to keep my head down
And savor the flavor
Of mint
Or salt
Or sweat licked straight from the forehead
I enjoy solitude and the sunset
Because it's beautiful
Not because I love the night

Advice Podcasts

Listening to podcasts
On my back on this dock
It's too cold and cloudy to be wearing a bathing suit
And for nonexistent advice
On this nonexistent day
I'm looking for satisfaction in all the wrong places
Exhaustion
Is that it?
Dissociation
Is that what it's called
When there are bags under my eyes
As dark as
Well nothing
Nothing is that dark here
But I swear I've slept for months
I swear
I'm happy
As my sentences get shorter and shorter
And my arguments less and less convincing
Eat and sleep and fuck and feel
I am looking for satisfaction in all the wrong places
Too cold for a swimsuit
But too warm for this sweatshirt
And sandals
The ferry is coming
Maybe you saw how empty I was
And maybe that's why
You so badly needed me to be full
But I am looking for satisfaction

In all the wrong places
Maybe if I can't be full
I'll fill myself like you did
With sweetness and richness
To drown out any doubts
I don't miss her
I would say that's why I prefer bitterness to sugar
But that wouldn't be accounting for
The years before I met you
So maybe I chose you
Because you felt like the emptiness I already had
And I needed a reason
To feel it

Bright Blue

My room smells like lilies
And the new flesh smell
Of right after a shower
If I close my eyes in the morning
On the small porch of my room
And drink orange juice straight from the jug
With my face to the sun
I'm almost satisfied with myself
My neck seems like it always hurts these days
But it's more of a phantom pain
Then anything
Another thing I've learned,
You can't cry to reggae
As I braid my hair and take pictures of dead fish
In grey muddy water
I personally love this narrator
But I've been told it lacks power
Which is really
The epitome of irony

One of my pillows has a blood stain on it
And I am shaking
Shaking
Shaking with anticipation
There's nothing like a luke warm shower after the ocean
And I think I prefer salt bleached to sun
Sometimes you can tell when someone's had sex
I think I act that way

After skating

I have never felt cleaner, and maybe more pure
In my life
An artist
Collecting bones and jumping off docks
Fully clothed
If I was happy all the time I'd never be happy
Happily ever after
How awful is that?

I'm eating flesh and drinking honey
With gods and monsters
Wearing nothing but my all black underwear
And stringy hair
Alone on the beach

My bathroom light is out
So I use a flashlight to shower

On My Stomach

Everyone is awake and listening to Kendrick Lamar
On their stomachs in bed
Everyone is awake
With their eyes closed
I don't want to disappear
Even though all my fantasies
Involve dissolving
I don't want to go backwards
No matter how warm the broth was
In contrast to my freezing feet
In contrast to the mold stains on the mattress
I know what I want
But it's good knowing
They still want me home

Simple pleasures
How can I love so many things and still feel nothing?
I just want to turn the speaker down
While we walk past kids playing in their yards
In the middle of summer
I don't love anyone else like that

Moving on is the decomposition of life

The growth of a seed
Must be painful
It has to uncurl
From where it felt safe and warm

Just to be burnt by the sun
Like the backs of my legs
On my stomach
On the surfboard
The water tasted better than you did
I know what I want

But it's nice knowing
They still want me home

So many people write love poems
And that's just beyond me
The times I've been in love
No words could describe
Or be as beautiful
And I didn't want to write anyways

How could I forget what I did to you?

On my stomach
Because my back hurts so bad
How can I feel so many things
Without feeling anything at all?

My favorite pastime is listening through doors
Without caring what they say
I wonder if you kept it

My love poem

Convenience Store Rush Hour

Fast walking as the sun goes down
With a whole loaf of bread
And a speaker in my back pocket
"Drink coffee god damn you"
And stop sleeping on that mattress
A welcome mat for discomfort
I bought coconut flakes from a man who spoke perfect English
And was so surprised
All I said was "efcharistó"
And laughed at myself the whole way home
The definition of foreboding
Is when it's so windy the waters are calm
Last time it rained
I was wearing corduroy pants
With a deck of cards and a mug of soup
I probably should've said goodbye

Wet Cats

Too much wine makes you feel like family
As I write poetry about four walls
While lying backwards in bed
Maybe I found myself
Or maybe I finally got lost
Now my fingers smell like dill and lemon
Today's word is dampness
And wet cats
And metal tables dragged over cobblestones
Set in the middle of kitchens
So they can still smoke and pretend they're outside
I eat trail mix with a spoon
And stand in puddles in sandals
Pulling out fist fulls of hair and smiling
Because sometimes lately
I forget to exist
The only customer in this restaurant
Under a big white umbrella
I cut my hands on my keys
And stain the wall with pomegranate juice
Juxtaposition
Is the key to beauty
Desirability
Irony
And life

Dissociation Sickness

Hands covered in pollen
And sheets covered in blood
Three women barely wrapped in bedclothes
Hanging on the wall
Doves perched on power lines, above burning trash
White smoke and a white men's shirt
That comes unbuttoned
As I run around corners chased by cars
Cat's cradle
Cat and mouse
Pussy wants a corner

Cats got my tongue
But I find solace in silence, and this conceptual landscape
Inhabited by nuns wearing headlamps
And potbellied men
This little clay hillside
Covered in fallen pomegranates
Rotting and eaten by bees
Milk and honey and supermarket rabbits feet
Pure white and speckled with blood
Every culture has a purging
A great undoing, a flood
I have a flooded bedroom
When I wake up at 2am to watch the lightning
Is this comfort?

I am in love with the weight on my back
And a pack mule never complains
Hands covered in pollen
I remember ripping at the heads of fish with my teeth
These are my rituals
Pulling teeth one by one
So someday I will speak clearly through this dry throat
Through this unnecessary imagery
Like uneven floors
And boats on the water
And gods with heavy hands
A pack of cigarettes washes up on the beach
Maybe Icarus was smoking
Is there really a difference
Between tending a wound and tending a flock?
Consensual freedom
I've been convinced this whole time
That good posture and a strong back
Make a racehorse
But what does it say
That all the women who raised me
Idolize gay men?

Claustrophobia and other Desires

Sweating through my sweater
Sleeves rolled up
Bracelet indents on my wrists
Welcoming the pain in my mouth
Biting down
My earbuds bounce on my chest
Uneven ground
As I write my obituary
But refuse to dig my own grave
Fake poetry
I can't see through the hair in my eyes
Crushing small flowers under my feet
And buying tickets to concerts in my hometown
I know I'll never go to
There's no wind
Just the open ocean and the Flaming Lips
To serenade me along the beach
With broken feet I'll never stop walking
Someone else's heart written in the sand
Crushed under my feet
I'll never stop walking
Skin tight
Across my fingers
I couldn't get the ring off if I wanted to
And it smells like home here
So maybe I won't get back before dark
The secret to adversity
Is making eye contact
Bared teeth are easily mistaken as a smile

And the winds back
And I'm walking backwards
But in no way retracing my steps
As two shirtless men wrestle to the ground
And help each other up
And smile
With bared teeth
Two canaries and seven cats
I wonder who they feed the scraps to
This morning I took fingernails to my skin
In an attempt to shed it

Hometown

My jacket was covered in gasoline stains
He pulled my braids
And I fell backwards in bed
Even with someone else's arms around me
I tried to take the knife from your fist
Prying apart white knuckles
That was love
It was raining
And all you wanted was a bong hit under the bridge
We were supposed to be watching fireworks
But instead I stumbled along at his uneven pace
And convinced you not to
I can remember the smell of that basement
And how hard we had to concentrate down the stairs
Damp from sweat and rain and mildew
Even then
I remember my heart sinking
At the number of bodies on the bed
And the blood
On my lips
As I hid the knife in my back pocket

Cyclades

Watching Quinten Tarantino movies
And drinking a homemade cocktail
Feeling fancy with a lime perched on the rim
Everything is clear
Fresh squeezed lemon juice
The horizon
It's easy to be honest with yourself
Rather than cutting through farmland
And ducking under barbed wire fences
Like I was raised on

We wander through the compounds
Of gated communities
Fiddling with padlocks
And passing by pools I so badly want to jump in
Fully clothed
There's no one else here
But some gardeners on the hill
Rippling at the edges
Like spirits or shadows, from long dead myths
Pushing wheelbarrows full
Of designer stones

Goodbyes

Stomach noises
Showering in the dark
Happy with the fact I'm useable
But not untouchable
My desire to runway
I've worn these clothes and drank from these bottles
It might be time to throw them out
I stood outside next to olive trees
And clay pots in the moonlight
And rambled on and on
Waiting
I used to want to marry everything
To be everything
Permanently
Now I savor nonexistent days and paper bags of pastries
And hot coffee, and mold stains, and making long eye contact
Knowing I'll never look back
I don't need to play that song anymore
To remind myself
It's okay not to say goodbye
And all those dreams about disappearing
Were really just metaphors for closed doors
Who knew opportunity tasted so sweet
And denial so bitter
But I love black coffee and red wine
And don't care so much anymore
There're coins in my wallet

They rattle when I walk
And blisters between my toes
Tomorrow I'll go swimming
Even if it rains
And get things done and wake up late
Like the good little machine I am
My hand is cramping
It has for days
And I'm sick of picking up and settling down
Now content with just looking
And nursing a wound
Like the baby mouse in that cardboard box
We all knew would die anyways

Zodiacs

Dinner at 5pm
They ordered lattes
Which were not on the menu
And she ordered white wine
I ordered a black coffee
Like always
Which wasn't on the menu either
They talked about horoscopes
And I thought it was funny
Because I didn't believe, yet just earlier I'd thought
How fitting our drinks are
In explaining our lives

Politics

What did I do this winter?
I learned to shut up
Sitting cross legged on a dock in the dark
Lit by a string of Christmas lights
And a bottle of ouzo set on an iPhone screen
Playing cards
And politics
The water wasn't as cold as I expected
When we all jumped in on the bass drop
Of Tov Lo's Habits Stay High
The Hippie Sabotage remix
I was still wearing a t-shirt
Because it'd been too warm for a bra
And the strings were unraveling
The sand was soft, as I ducked under boat ties
And she took her bra off
Because that girl just can't pass up a chance
To get naked
Walking back they played their trance playlist
And I watched the way
The water glittered on the sand
The next night on Santorini
They yelled at me
And threw shoes
Because I didn't feel like going out
And preferred Chinese food
I learned later on
They got kicked out of the bar
And kept myself from smiling

Convoluted

Who am I without this guilt?
I guess that's what I needed
To destroy
I'm always amazed
By my capacity for self-destruction
So what can I do but scratch these mosquito bites
And listen to the Cranberries when my feet get cold
This is what I've always wanted
No matter how convoluted it got
And I'm almost out of paper
Already
Today I'll drink coffee while it's too hot
And find somewhere to sit
And write pie charts
Because I'm young and dumb and

Lying to myself

Leaving Scissors in Greece

There's a steeple in the back of that pickup
As I try on the skin I wanted to wear
Even if it doesn't fit yet
My feet are blistered in anticipation
And catching a glimpse in the mirror
My face is red
This is ankles bitten by mosquitos
And tongues bitten by teeth
Looking over my shoulder
While fighting my way forwards
Through waist deep water
This is looking at rocks and seeing my reflection
Cold and hard as stone
And learning to love negative space
Without missing what used to fill it
Carrying winter inside me
While chasing summer across time zones
And loving the finality of things cleaned with bleach
Living in airports because I'm temporary
And elated by the fact my room is as empty
As I want to be

Poems about Cigarettes and Coffee

Guilty mornings
Dolmas for breakfast
Fully clothed and force feeding myself
While wiping blood from my cracked screen
And wooden door frame
Apparently I'm an optimist
After two liters of wine
In two metal cups
And two cafes playing Cyndi Lauper
Girls Just Want To Have Fun
I am counting the days like this one
With three gold coins in my pencil bag
But only writing in blue pen
My hands still cold and my cheeks still warm
I said if the world came to an end tomorrow
I wouldn't have cared
And for once in my life
I meant it

No More Peacetime

Am I growing or dying?
Conflict
I'm desperately decomposing
Hoping
That whatever grows from my filth
Is prettier than I ever was
And twice as fierce
My brain may be rotting
But rotten fruit is sweet
And essential for wine and other spirits
Giving me more than one way to run from my problems
While dragging them behind me
Like a bunch of tin cans
But no one can hear my racket
And my only consolation
Is that silence is more menacing
Then any half assed sound
There's two inches of water on my bedroom floor
And a stick of convenience store incense
Balanced on my bedside table
Under the remote for a TV that has never worked
I'm wearing shoes in bed
And murdering time
Because killing sounds so passive
And I'm not messing around

Long Distance Holiday

I woke up freezing in the Mediterranean
And burned my crumpled lists and routines
To keep warm
It's strange to wake up on a day that means nothing
And long to say goodbye before its time
Because the winds are back and I'm sick of squinting
When I can remember feeling at peace
I recite clichés I wish I didn't relate to
And buy a loaf of fresh bread
And homemade jam
To share in the absence of emotional resources
They've been drilling for this whole time
And I don't know why everyone is so in love
With everything
The smell of cooked meat is tantalizing
But someone said recently
That we should all be vegetarian
So I'd rather save my coins for coffee
Because I get so cold at night
I do love sweaters and twisted ankles
And I've gotten so good at lying
With just my eyes
But nothing lasts forever
And half of me has already been sent away
I hate that I know where I belong

Art Show Weekend

She laughs too loud
But it's okay because we're celebrating
In the tiny corner booth
Of a greasy Greek bar
Where our double order of fries and wine and coffee
Is paid for by the next table over
While I open up out of necessity
To temporary families and the last few days
Of grey skies and unsure timelines
The mental jetlag of anticipation
Walking home from breakfast at 1pm
To the smell of fresh olive oil
And lipstick stains on a small ceramic cup
Of Greek coffee
I stood in the corner of the art show
With a paper cup full of red wine
And talked about the enjoyment of dry reading
And white washed bones
I feel like I do everything backwards
Eating soup from a frying pan
And working out in my underwear
At 2am
This is my uneven trajectory
Of tight jeans and flushed cheeks
That I never wanted
And climbing through bathroom windows
In full makeup
That I never usually wear
Downloading the smooth jazz playlist

By Spotify
Because someone asked for background music
And I never know what to play
Wondering if you have to be self-absorbed to be an artist
Or an alcoholic
Or if my constant self-destruction
And conflict
Could be love

Meal Times

There are some things even three sticks of cheap incense
Can't fix
Some mornings when getting dressed
Means changing out of last night's clothes
And into pajamas
At 2pm
Returning to my constant state of movement
From a brief inquiry into the static
Meal times mean nothing
And there's holes in my socks
Leaving me elated
With the knowledge that tomorrow I'll sleep in a different bed

Tell me how much you miss me

I demand
While the TV plays in Arabic
And I lay spread eagle on the bed
Wearing nothing but a bathrobe
And chains around my feet
Tell me how much you miss me
So I can look away
And marvel in my cruelty
Tell me how much you miss me
I beg
To empty walls and open spaces
Tell me how much you miss me
So I can finally run away

Six Hour Bath on a Twelve-Hour Layover

1.

Overflowing hotel bathtubs
I escape reality
By rubbing olive oil on my skin
In an airport parking lot
My viciousness is my lover
And I am melting into this ceramic tub
Sunning myself like a lizard on wet towels
The luxury of wet towels
Do not disturb
I can breathe again
My stomach is rumbling
But I can't afford another five-star meal
And seem to have lost the keys to the mini fridge
I love being sober
My skin is a different color with the dirt scrubbed off
And the smell of other people's sweat
I start a new novel but watch the same TV
This could be eternity
Because one of my ankle bracelets is missing
And with a promise to call I power off my phone
And enjoy
The fullness
Of my double bed mattress
And finally my clean
Conscious

2.

What do I want?
Right now
I want to paint a picture
To prove how I well I fit
Into this landscape
I want
To sit up straight and smile and use my knife and fork accordingly
And understand the seven languages on TV
But really I want
To finally wash my hair
To rip at my scalp with my fingernails
Till all my denial comes loose
And my perpetual pain feels something other
Then ordinary
Even if it makes me vulnerable
Alone in this empty room
I really
Am nothing but a chaotic stack of printed emails
And a dark green cargo bag
There're three socks on the hotel room floor
And it's beyond me how they got there
Because I can't feel my feet
I am shedding
Skin and dirt and guilt and responsibility
And my skateboard lies
Four feet from the bed
On the floor without wheels
I can't move

I want
To look through my backpack
Tearing at the seams
For the nicest shirt I own and the cleanest pair of underwear
Because god I'm hungry
And it's been so long
Since I was full

Birth

Crying for a tragedy
That never happened
Over a three course Indian meal
From a server who thanked me profusely
When I tipped him five bucks
My dream vacation
Staring at the wall
To the same album and cold shower
In a different hotel room
This is freedom
Walking myself to death
Knowing the bar will be closed when I reach it
Knowing they won't let me in
And I don't want to get there anyways
Why are there no trees?
I want to hide in the undergrowth
Like an old cat
Finding a place die
I wonder if birth is painful

Forgiveness

Three cardboard boxes in the trash
And the remainder of a chai latte
I'd rather forget
The way I tried to be someone else
My body is caving in one me
And I have never felt so beautiful
My feet are cut and bleeding
From dull nails
And my back aches
From the unnecessary weight I choose to carry
I see stars in the shower and blame the soap
And biting down has never been easier
Indulgent

That's what I am
My calloused ankles
Are the most beautiful thing I've seen
As I hide behind what I'm not
So I don't have to be what I am
I turned off the TV
But I still can't hear my heartbeat
And my knees pop when I stand
Did I hide behind the mess or the cleanliness?
I've learned to smile like an idiot
When no one's watching
But I still can't make eye contact
And I feel sick
With the rich food in my stomach
And my hands numb

When I was little
My dad told me to make a safe place
In my mind
A house just the way I liked it
Where nothing could get me
So I locked the door and tore myself to pieces

PDA

The bathroom smells like cinnamon
And the open door hits the bed
I don't regret my regrettable decisions
I want to feel beautiful again
And to stop writing
I want to be something other
Then this worn pair of sweatpants
And growling stomach and empty hands
The room is small and the bed is big
And once again
The romance is lost on me
I have done such a good job
Shrinking myself
That maybe someday
I will finally stop existing
I pulled my sweater below the wrists
And leaned on railings when I got too tired
They call each other 'princess' when they walk by
And I hang my head without looking away
What am I doing here?

Recovery is Just as Painful

Baptism in a hotel tub
I taste blood again
Finally clean
Buying travel sized toothpaste
And a razor
With Costa Rican money
At an American store
In Greece
The cocktail menus says
There's something for every mood
But I have always preferred
Silence

Hunger

I can't focus my eyes
They're dry from not blinking
And screaming
Something I've learned to tune out
And I'm still surprised
When I overhear conversations
I eat too quickly to enjoy it
And walk too fast to get anywhere on time
My coats too thin and my shoes too tight
And I wake up on the wrong side of the bed
I asked who I would be without this guilt
I am empty

Half Full

I guess you can romanticize anything
Numb hands and a cardboard box of Chinese food
Alone in the park
Drink water, feel guilty
Going in circles
Why does everything always hurt
Why don't I know if I enjoy it
I left
And come back with a book of chicken scratch
And a list of strange desires
I left and came back
With bruised feet and empty eyes
I came back and buried myself
In white sheets and a black shirt
I am contrast and contentment
Convincing myself
I can't be okay
The fear is gone
And I am terrified
Running to the ground
In chipped nail polish and a half full water bottle
Half full, half empty
Does it matter anymore
Cracked teeth and cracked fingertips
Fracture lines
I walk through the door with a yellow paper bag
A large coffee
Toothpaste and a bag of popcorn
Empty handed

From the animal farm to the slaughter house
Standing in the hallway
Elevator or stairs?
I have never been one to explode
Is it trauma or am I trauma?
They have always loved you
I am tired of running

Addiction

A white cup now empty
Full of coffee grounds
And a woman who can't help but order seconds
So she can stay in the cafe
I contemplate the nature of dependence
And it's connection
To addiction
And love
Both have negative connotations
Where you're free
And I've been disappearing too long
I need to fill these empty spaces
Sleeping through plans I used to depend on
There are six coins in my back pocket
And I don't know if they will buy me a train ticket
But I wear two sweaters just in case
I cried for the first time in two months
And didn't mean to stop
I eat only the crust off the piece of toast in front of me
And think
This is growing up